Contents

Reading words with digraphs and trigraphs

Two letters that go together to make one sound are called a digraph. Three letters that go together to make one sound are called a trigraph.

 snail ●　●　──　●

 hair ●　──

▶ Look for the digraphs or trigraphs in these words. Draw a line under them. Use sound-talk to read the words and tick the word that goes with the picture.

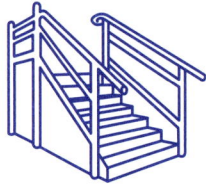 stairs ☐　　　stars ☐

 sleep ☐　　　scoop ☐

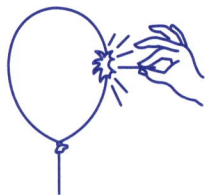 bright ☐　　　burst ☐

 flower ☐　　　float ☐

 strain ☐　　　storm ☐

▶ Use sound-talk to read these words. Draw the sound buttons as you say the sounds. Join each word to the correct picture.

paint

● — ● ●

spear

toast

thrush

spoon

marching

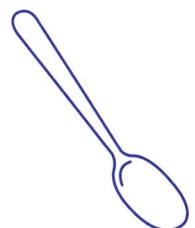

Reading words ending -est

► This two-part word has **–est** added on the end. Use sound-talk to read the word. Be careful. The **–est** ending is not said exactly the same as how you sound-talk it.

soft**est**

► Read each caption. Tick the picture that goes with the caption.

the brightest star ☐ ☐

the steepest ramp ☐ ☐

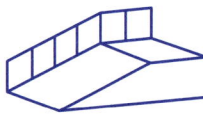

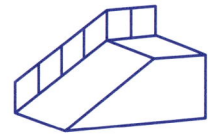

the sharpest point ☐ ☐

the smoothest string ☐ ☐

the darkest hair ☐ ☐

Schofield & Sims · **My Letters and Sounds**

Reading words ending –ed

▶ These words have **–ed** added on the end. Use sound-talk to read the words. Be careful. The **–ed** ending is not always said exactly the same way. Sometimes you cannot hear the /e/ sound.

start**ed**   stain**ed**

▶ Read each sentence and the two words next to or below it. Choose the word that makes sense in the sentence and draw a ring round it.

A dog ____ at it.   growled   groaned

An owl ____ at it.   hooted   hunted

Someone ____ at it.   painted   pointed

The children ____ to run with it.

snarled   started

A red balloon ____ up and up.

floated   fainted

▶ Read the tricky word. Look out for the tricky parts.

love

● ● —

▶ Read each question. Write **yes** or **no**.

Do you love cricket? _____

Do you love cartoons? _____

Do frogs love to swim? _____

Do dogs love thunder? _____

Do you love to sleep? _____

Do you love the rain? _____

Do children love sweets? _____

▶ Read the tricky word. Look out for the tricky part.

look*ed*

▶ Read the sentences. Join each sentence to the correct picture.

The king lost his crown.
He looked cross.

He looked up on the
highest shelf.

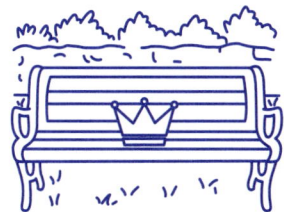

He looked under the
stairs.

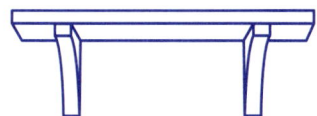

He looked in the
chest.

He looked in the garden.
There it was.

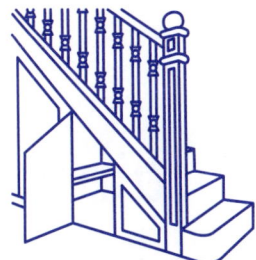

The digraph ay

▶ These two letters together make the **/ai/** sound. Say the sound.

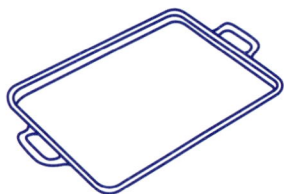

tr**ay**

ay

⋯⋯⋯⋯⋯⋯⋯⋯⋯⋯⋯⋯⋯⋯⋯⋯⋯⋯⋯⋯⋯⋯⋯⋯⋯⋯⋯

▶ Read the sentences. Draw a line under the digraph **ay**.
Join each sentence to the correct picture.

I have some soft clay.

Press to spray.

What a lot of hay!

There is one crayon.

It rained today.

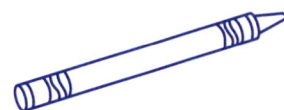

Read each clue and the answers below it. Draw a ring round the correct answer.

This is what you do in a shop.

paint	pray	pay

This is what trees do in the wind.

stay	sway	way

This is what you might say to a dog.

stray	stay	spray

This is what children love to do.

play	prowl	pay

This is what a hen might do.

fray	say	lay

The digraph ou

▶ These two letters together make the **/ow/** sound. Say the sound.

 cloud

ou

▶ Use sound-talk to read the two words on each line. Draw a line under the digraph **ou**. Tick the word that goes with the picture.

 proud ☐   pound ☐

 sprouts ☐   spout ☐

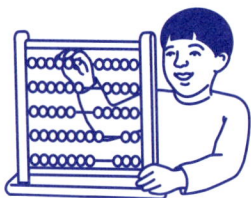 count ☐   clout ☐

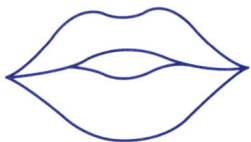 mount ☐   mouth ☐

 fairground ☐   playground ☐

► Say the words in sound-talk. All of the words have an **/ow/** sound that is spelt **ou**. Write in the letters needed to complete each word.

ou	t	

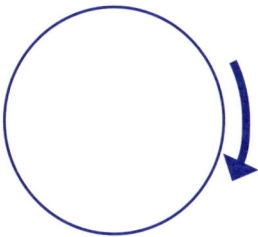

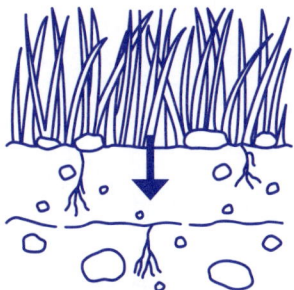

The digraph ie

▶ These two letters together make the **/igh/** sound. Say the sound.

 p*ie*

ie

▶ Use sound-talk to read these words. Draw the sound buttons as you say the sounds. Join each word to the correct picture.

tie

fries

magpie

lie

flies

▶ Read each sentence and the two words below it. Choose the word that makes sense in the sentence and write it on the line.

I _____ one magpie.

spied   cries

The flowers have all _____.

dries   died

The string was _____ round.

tied   tries

She _____ some of the pie.

tried   tied

Do you like _____ eggs?

dried   fried

"Get out of the way," he _____.

spied   cried

▶ Read the tricky word.

oh

▶ Read the speech bubbles. Join each speech bubble to the correct picture.

Oh dear, I have lost my sheep.

Oh Gran, what big teeth you have!

Oh no! Someone is sleeping in my bed.

Oh, I am way too quick for you.

► Read the tricky word. Look out for the tricky parts.

people

► Read each question. Write **yes** or **no**.

Do people lie on clouds? _____

Can people feel proud? _____

Do people have mouths? _____

Do all people love sprouts? _____

Can some people play chess? _____

Do some people love
fried fish? _____

The digraph ea

▶ These two letters together make the **/ee/** sound. Say the sound.

 s**ea**

e**a**

▶ Use sound-talk to read the three words on each line.
Draw a ring round the word that goes with the picture.

 pies pays peas

 steam stream seat

 peach pouch peak

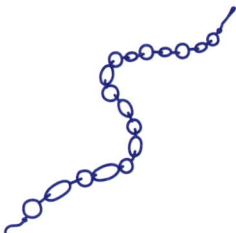 beads beans beats

 teacher teabag teapot

Schofield & Sims · **My Letters and Sounds**

Say the words in sound-talk. All of the words have an **/ee/** sound that is spelt **ea**. Write in the letters needed to complete each word.

l	ea	f

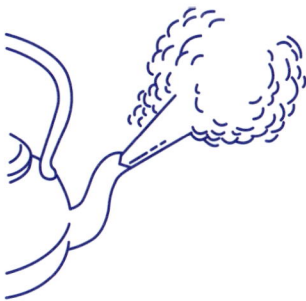

The digraph oy

▶ These two letters together make the **/oi/** sound. Say the sound.

 b**oy**

oy

......

▶ Read the sentences. Draw a line under the digraph **oy**.
Join each sentence to the correct picture.

Jump for joy.

I have some toy cars.

He shouts, "Ship ahoy!"

Troy was a cowboy.

"Oh no!" says Roy.

Do you enjoy reading? _____

Do some people annoy you? _____

Do you enjoy cowboy films? _____

Do loud sounds annoy you? _____

Do some boys enjoy toys? _____

Do you enjoy playing sport? _____

Can a squeak be annoying? _____

The digraph ir

▶ These two letters together make the **/ur/** sound. Say the sound.

 b**ir**d

ir

▶ Use sound-talk to read the two words on each line. Draw a line under the digraph **ir**. Draw a ring round the word that goes with the picture.

   first   third

   girl   sir

   squirt   shirt

13   thirst   thirteen

   Thursday   birthday

What has a beak and chirps?

a girl ☐   a boy ☐   a blackbird ☐

What has arms and buttons?

a skirt ☐   a shirt ☐   shorts ☐

What do people do with a spoon?

speak ☐   count ☐   stir ☐

What is a sort of grin?

a smirk ☐   a squirt ☐   a twirl ☐

What can be found on the ground?

dart ☐   firm ☐   dirt ☐

▶ Read the tricky word. Look at the tricky parts. Then copy the word.

some _____ _____ _____

....

▶ Look at the pictures. Write the tricky word **some** and the other missing word to complete each caption.

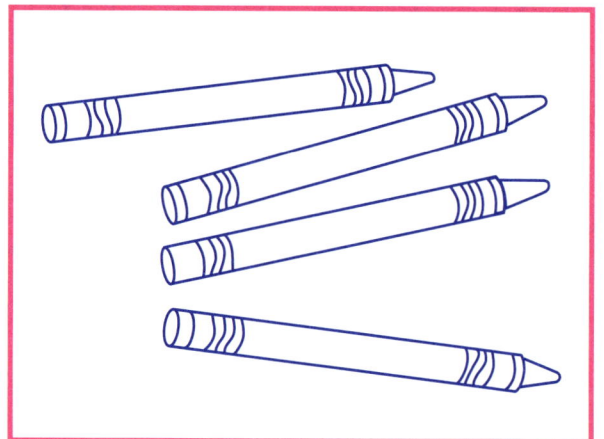

some steam _____ _____

► Read the tricky word. Look at the tricky parts. Then copy the word.

come _____ _____ _____

► Write the tricky word **some** or **come** to complete each sentence.

_____ out of there.

_____ girls tried to help.

Can you _____ out to play?

We found _____ red beads.

_____ and enjoy the beach.

_____ and read to the teacher.

▶ Read the tricky word. Look out for the tricky part.

their
———

··

▶ Read each sentence and the three words below it. Choose the word that makes sense in the sentence and write it on the line.

People stir their _____.

thirst   tea   tie

Children play with their _____.

trays   ties   toys

The peach was out of their _____.

reach   real   read

The crowd shout for their _____.

team   treat   teach

The twins enjoyed their _____.

bird   dirt   birthday

▶ Read the tricky word. Look out for the tricky part.

y**our**

● ___

▶ Read the sentences. Finish the picture to go with each sentence.

Have some cream on your pie.

Have some peas with your meat.

You can have fries with your burger.

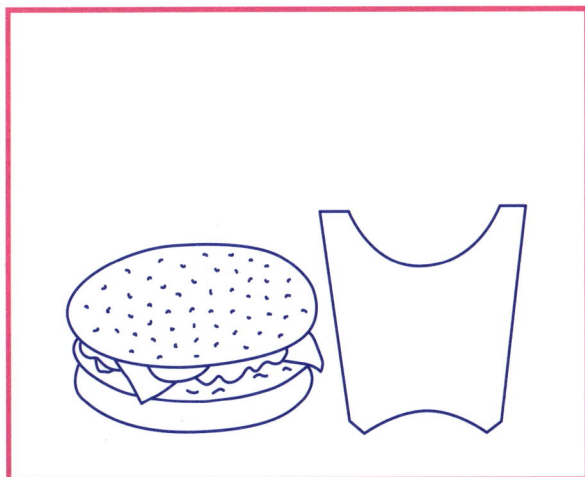

Have a drink of tea with your meal.

The digraph aw

▶ These two letters together make the **/or/** sound. Say the sound.

 sees**aw**

aw

▶ Use sound-talk to read the two words on each line. Draw a line under the digraph **aw**. Tick the word that goes with the picture.

 shirt ☐   shawl ☐

 stray ☐   straw ☐

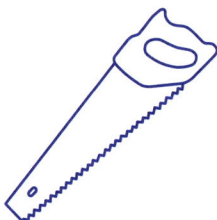 saw ☐   jaw ☐

 laws ☐   lawn ☐

 drawing ☐   dawn ☐

► Say the words in sound-talk. All of the words have an **/or/** sound that is spelt **aw**. Write in the letters needed to complete each word.

y	aw	n

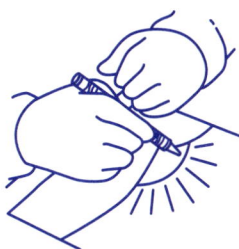

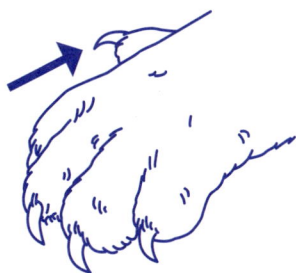

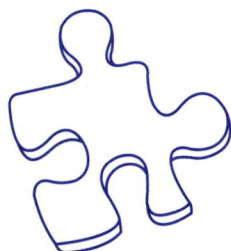

The digraph ue

▶ These two letters together make the **/oo/** or **/yoo/** sound. Say the sound.

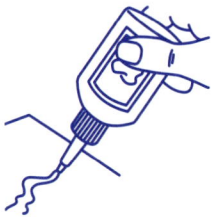 glue    barbecue   **ue**

▶ Use sound-talk to read these words. Draw the sound buttons as you say the sounds. Join each word to the correct picture.

Sue

bluebell

argue

statue

blue

This is your first clue. _____

Your shirt is blue. _____

All statues stand still. _____

Your birthday is on Tuesday. _____

Some people like to argue. _____

You play snooker with a cue. _____

Boats like this rescue people. _____

The digraph ew

▶ These two letters together make the **/oo/** or **/yoo/** sound. Say the sound.

 bl**ew**    n**ew**s   **ew**

▶ Read the sentences. Draw a line under the digraph **ew**. Join each sentence to the correct picture.

I saw dew on a leaf.

I found one screw.

Your stew smells good.

I like their new car.

I have a few stickers.

▶ Read each sentence and the three words below it. Choose the
word that makes sense in the sentence and write it on the line.

The north wind _____.

drew   blue   blew

Their sunflower _____.

glue   grew   screw

All the birds _____ away.

few   threw   flew

I _____ a girl and a boy.

drew   dew   dawn

The cows _____ their hay.

stew   brew   chew

Andrew joined the _____.

chew   crew   screw

▶ Read the tricky words. Look at the tricky parts. Then copy the words.

said _____   so _____

▶ Write the tricky words **said** and **so** to complete each sentence.

They _____ the pie was _____ good.

It was true, or _____ he _____ .

Dawn _____ the sea looked _____ blue.

"You tried _____ hard," _____ the teacher.

Lewis _____ your lawn is _____ green.

"I am _____ proud of you," _____ Dad.

▶ Read the tricky word. Look at the tricky part. Then copy the word.

have _____ _____ _____

▶ Look at the pictures. Write the tricky word **have** and the other missing word to complete each sentence.

Birds __have__ __beaks__.

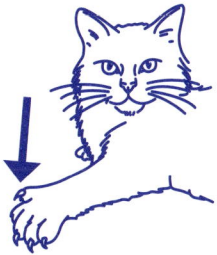
Cats _____ _____.

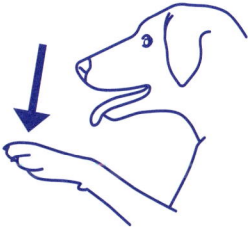
Dogs _____ _____.

Mouths _____ _____.

Teapots _____ _____.

▶ Read the tricky words.

Mr   Mrs

▶ Read the sentences. Then colour the picture using the correct colours.

Mr Renfrew has
a new blue shirt.

Mrs Floyd has
a green skirt and
a blue shawl.

Mr Renfrew has
a black beard.

Mrs Floyd tries
on her new red hat.

▶ Read the sentences. Join each sentence to the correct picture.

Mr Boyd reads the clues.

Mr Mount loves to draw.

Mrs Kirk tries a new sport.

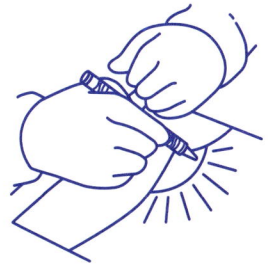

Mr Shaw collects toy cars.

Mrs Drew flew to Spain.

Mrs Day grew beans
and peas.

The digraph oe

▶ These two letters together make the **/oa/** sound. Say the sound.

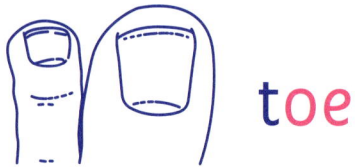

toe

oe

▶ Read the sentences. Draw a line under the digraph **oe**.
  Join each sentence to the correct picture.

Joe stands on tiptoe.

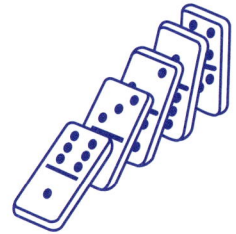

A balloon goes pop.

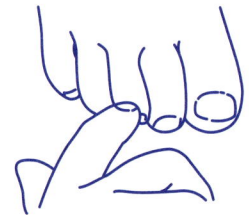

Count your toes.

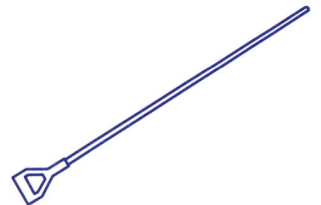

We play dominoes.

Pick up the garden hoe.

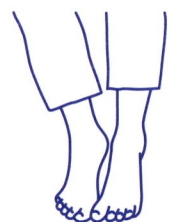

▶ These two letters together make the **/or/** sound. Say the sound.

 Paul

au

. . . .

▶ Use sound-talk to read these words. Draw the sound buttons as you say the sounds. Join each word to the correct picture.

Maud

launch

haunted

daub

August

The split digraph i-e

▶ These two letters together make the **/igh/** sound. This is called a split digraph because the two letters are not right next to each other. Say the sound.

 kite

i-e

▶ Use sound-talk to read the three words on each line. Draw a line to join the two letters in the split digraph **i-e**. Draw a ring round the word that goes with the picture.

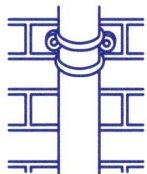 pile   pipe   prize

 fine   first   fire

 side   slide   smile

 bike   bird   bite

 tile   team   time

► Look at the pictures. Write the word **like** and the other missing word or words to complete each sentence.

I ___like___ going for a ___drive___ .

I _____ playing on my _____ .

I _____ having a day at the sea_____ .

I _____ to _____ my _____ .

I _____ to win first _____ .

Reading tricky words **asked** and **called**

▶ Read the tricky words. Look out for the tricky parts.

ask   asked

● ● ●   ● ● ● ——

▶ Read each sentence and the three words below it. Choose the word that makes sense in the sentence and write it on the line.

Ask Mr Clive what _____ it is.

nine   time   five

He asked if the room was _____.

haunted   hunted   hauled

Ask if you can have three _____.

toes   jaws   goes

Paula asked for a ride on my _____.

book   bike   beak

Mike asked to play hide and _____.

side   slide   seek

▶ Read the tricky words. Look out for the tricky parts.

call   called

• • —   • • — —

▶ Read the sentences. Join each sentence to the correct picture.

There was a little boy called Jay.

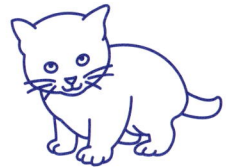

"Go away!" called the first little pig.

The king called for his slippers.

"Call for the rescue team!" she shouted.

"Come back!" they called.

They called the kitten Spike.

▶ These two letters together make the **/ai/** sound. Say the sound.

 cake

a-e

▶ Use sound-talk to read the two words on each line. Draw a line to join the two letters in the split digraph **a-e**. Draw a ring round the word that goes with the picture.

 gate   gaze

 fame   flame

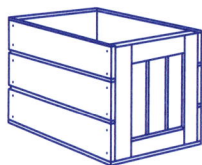 crate   craze

 pancake   snake

 cornflakes milkshake

▶ Say the words in sound-talk. All of the words have an **/ai/** sound that is spelt **a-e**. Write in the letters needed to complete each word.

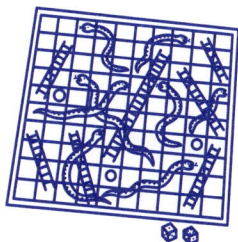

g	a	m	e

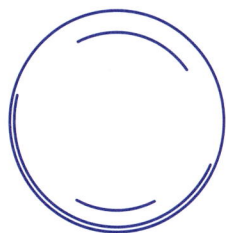

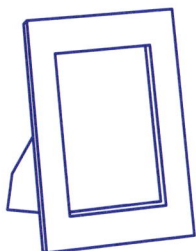

The split digraph o-e

▶ These two letters together make the **/oa/** sound. Say the sound.

 bone

o-e

▶ Use sound-talk to read these words. Draw the sound buttons as you say the sounds. Join each word to the correct picture.

nose

stone

note

smoke

rose

▶ Read each sentence and the three words below it. Choose the word that makes sense in the sentence and write it on the line.

The statue was made of _____.

stole   stone   cone

Dad was late so he called _____.

hose   home   throne

Mrs Rose drove down the _____.

pole   stroke   slope

Mr Deal was left all _____.

about   alone   alike

In the winter their pond _____.

broke   spoke   froze

He looked down into the _____.

hole   rope   hope

The split digraph **u-e**

▶ These two letters together make the **/oo/** or **/yoo/** sound. Say the sound.

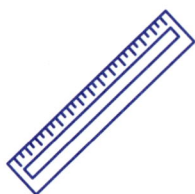 r**u**l**e**r   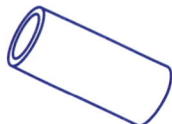 t**u**b**e**   u-e

▶ Read the sentences. Draw a line to join the two letters in the split digraph **u-e**. Join each sentence to the correct picture.

Mr Blake plays the flute.

Use this to rule a line.

Oh, what a cute kitten!

Do you love prunes?

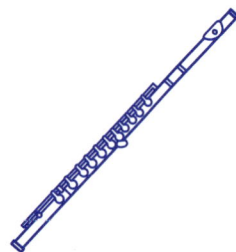

Turn up the volume.

Schofield & Sims · **My Letters and Sounds**

▶ Read each clue and the answers below it. Draw a ring round the correct answer.

A girl can be called this.

June   Luke   Dave

It is a shape with six sides.

a cub   a cube   a cone

Your toothpaste comes in it.

a tub   a tube   a dome

People can play a tune on this.

a flute   a fuse   a flake

You can turn this up or down.

fame   fortune   volume

▶ Read the tricky word. Look out for the tricky part.

could

● ━━━ ●

▶ Read each sentence. Tick the box if you think you could do it.

I could count to nineteen. ☐

I could bake you a cake. ☐

I could smile all the time. ☐

I could play you a tune. ☐

I could make up a game. ☐

I could tell you a good joke. ☐

I could ride my bike outside. ☐

would should

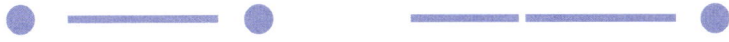

▶ Read each question. Write **yes** or **no**.

Would you crawl on thorns? _____

Would you stroke a snake? _____

Would your dog like a bone? _____

Should a king have a throne? _____

Should people smash plates? _____

Should you cross a road alone? _____

▶ Read the tricky word. Look at the tricky part. Then copy the word.

there _____ _____ _____

....

▶ Write the tricky words **there** and **they** to complete each sentence.

"Oh look, _____ is a cave," the children said.

"What is in _____?" _____ said.

_____ went and looked inside.

_____ was a dragon in _____.

"What are you doing _____?" _____ said.

► Read the tricky word. Look at the tricky part. Then copy the word.

were _____ _____ _____

► Write the tricky words **there**, **were** and the other missing word to complete each sentence. Finish the picture to go with each sentence.

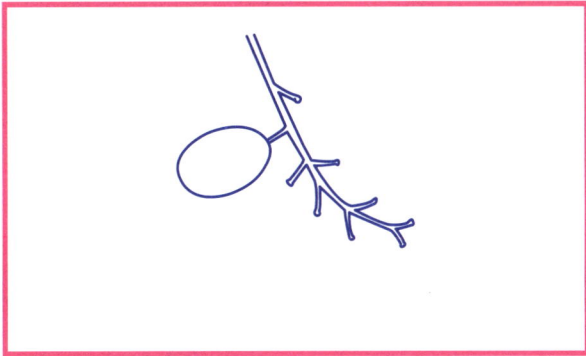

____There____ ____were____ nine grapes in the ____bunch____ .

_____ _____ three cakes on the _____ .

_____ _____ five birds on the _____ .

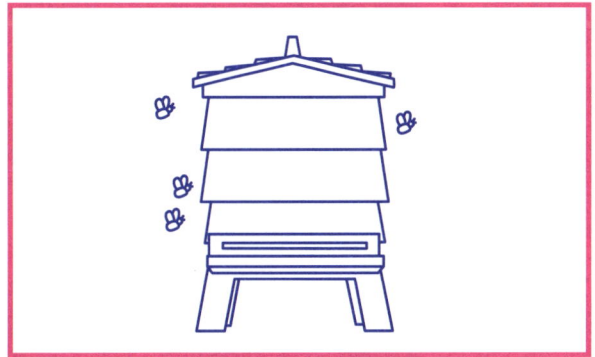

_____ _____ seven bees around their _____ .

The split digraph e-e

► These two letters together make the /ee/ sound. Say the sound.

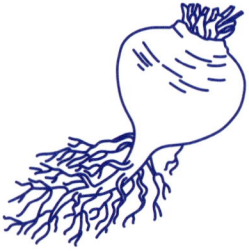 sw**e**d**e**

e-e

► Use sound-talk to read these words. Draw the sound buttons as you say the sounds. Join each word to the correct picture.

athlete

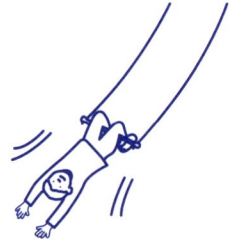

trapeze

Steve

theme park

Eve

Schofield & Sims · **My Letters and Sounds**

Would you visit a theme park? _____

Could you complete a jigsaw? _____

Have you met a boy
called Pete? _____

Would you like a go on
a trapeze? _____

Would you like to be
an athlete? _____

Do you have
crayons like these? _____

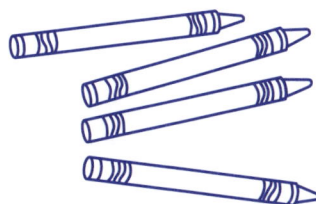

The digraph wh

▶ These two letters together make the **/w/** sound. Say the sound.

 **wh**eel

wh

▶ Use sound-talk to read the two words on each line. Draw a line under the digraph **wh**. Draw a ring round the word that goes with the picture.

   wheat   white

   while   whale

   whisk   whack

   whisker   whisper

   wheelchair   whirlpool

Read the questions and the possible answers. Write the missing word **which** or **when** to complete each question. Draw a ring round the correct answer.

Which of these has whiskers?

a snake   (a kitten)   a whale

_____ of these is round?

a wheel   a slope   a cube

_____ do birds wake up?

at dawn   in a while   on Tuesday

_____ of these is a shape?

white   a stone   a cone

_____ means to turn round?

wipe   whizz   whirl

The digraph ph

▶ These two letters together make the **/f/** sound. Say the sound.

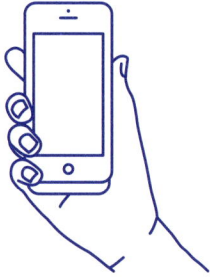

phone

ph

▶ Read the sentences. Draw a line under the digraph **ph**.
Join each sentence to the correct picture.

I saw a dolphin.

This is my phonics book.

Mrs Philips is a teacher.

I love my toy elephant.

Phew! It's so hot.

Which of these swim in the sea?

a whale	a phantom	an elephant
a seal	a hamster	a dolphin

Which of these would help you read?

wheels	phonics	the time
counters	teachers	the alphabet

Which of these could be names for boys?

Ralph	Steph	James
Eve	Jake	Kate

Which of these could you hold?

a phone	a note	a whisper
a whisk	a lake	a phantom

▶ Read the tricky words. Look out for the tricky part in the
second word.

our   here

_____   •   — _____

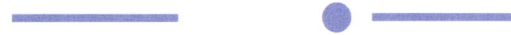

▶ Read the signs. Join each sign to the correct picture.

These are our
homemade cakes.

Here are our new
reading books.

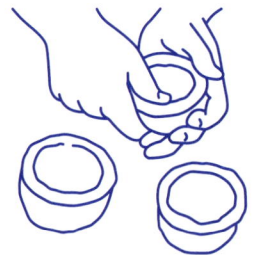

All our toys and
games are kept here.

Here are the clay
pots we made.

▶ Read the tricky words. Look out for the tricky parts.

house   mouse

▶ Read each question. Write **yes** or **no**.

Could a mouse ride a bike? _____

Can you ask a mouse to tea? _____

Would a mouse have whiskers? _____

Should I make a house
out of hay? _____

Have you ever seen
a lighthouse? _____

Is this house made
of straw?

_____

Phoneme families

More than one grapheme can represent a sound. The two graphemes **oi** and **oy** both make the **/oy/** sound.

▶ Write the other grapheme or graphemes for these sounds.

the **/ow/** sound   _____

the **/ur/** sound   _____

the **/w/** sound   _____

the **/f/** sound   _____

the **/ai/** sound   _____   _____

the **/igh/** sound   _____   _____

the **/ee/** sound   _____   _____

the **/or/** sound   _____   _____

the **/oa/** sound   _____   _____

the **/oo/** or **/yoo/** sound   _____   _____   _____

Schofield & Sims · **My Letters and Sounds**

Glossary

blend	to say the separate sounds in a word and merge them together to read the whole word. **Blending** is the reverse of **segmenting**.
digraph	two letters representing one sound (for example, 'ay')
grapheme	a letter or group of letters representing a **phoneme** or sound in a word
grapheme-phoneme correspondence (GPC)	matching a **phoneme** to a **grapheme**, and vice versa
phoneme	the smallest unit of sound in speech
phoneme family	a group of **graphemes** that represent the same sound (for example, the **graphemes** 'ai', 'ay', and 'a-e' represent the /ai/ **phoneme**)
segment	to break a word into separate sounds in order to spell it. **Segmenting** is the reverse of **blending**.
sound button	a mark appearing below each letter, **digraph** or **trigraph**, which the child can touch as they say the sound
sound-talk	the process of saying, in the correct order, each separate sound in a word
split digraph	two letters representing one sound, where the letters are not right next to each other (for example, the letters 'i' and 'e' in the word 'kite' form the **split digraph** 'i-e')
tricky word	a word that contains a letter or a group of letters that make an unusual or unfamiliar sound or a **grapheme** that the children do not yet know
trigraph	three letters representing one sound (for example, 'air')

Phonics Practice
Pupil Book 5

Schofield & Sims My Letters and Sounds is a comprehensive programme for teaching systematic synthetic phonics. Aligned with *Letters and Sounds*, it provides everything teachers and adult helpers need to teach reading with confidence.

The **My Letters and Sounds Phonics Practice Pupil Books** can be used in conjunction with the **My Letters and Sounds Teacher's Handbooks** to help support and embed learning.

Each book provides:

· **targeted practice** of each new learning point from **My Letters and Sounds**

· **integrated revision** of previous learning

· enjoyable, **age-appropriate activities**

· a helpful **glossary** of key phonic terms.

Phonics Practice Pupil Book 5 reinforces Phase Five, Term 1 of **My Letters and Sounds**. In this book, your child will revise the graphemes learnt in Reception, as well as being introduced to 18 new graphemes. Using the concept of 'phoneme families', they will be taught that a number of different graphemes can represent a given phoneme.

My Letters and Sounds coverage

Phase Two
Book 1

Phase Three
Book 2
Book 3

Phase Four
Book 4

Phase Five
Book 5
Book 6
Book 7
Book 8

My Letters and Sounds

Published by **Schofield & Sims Ltd**,
7 Mariner Court, Wakefield, West Yorkshire WF4 3FL, UK
Telephone 01484 607080
www.schofieldandsims.co.uk

This edition copyright © Schofield & Sims Ltd, 2022
First published in 2022

Author: **Carol Matchett**
Carol Matchett has asserted her moral rights under the Copyright, Designs and Patents Act, 1988, to be identified as the author of this work.

Phonics Consultant: **Jacqueline Harris**

British Library Cataloguing in Publication Data
A catalogue record for this book is available from the British Library.

Design by **Ledgard Jepson Ltd**
Cover design by **Ledgard Jepson Ltd**
Printed in the UK by **Page Bros (Norwich) Ltd**

For further information and to place your order visit www.schofieldandsims.co.uk or telephone 01484 607080

Schofield&Sims

ISBN 978-07217-1666-4

FSC
MIX
Paper from responsible sources
FSC® C023114

ISBN 978 0721 1666 4
£4.95 (Retail price)

9 780721 716664